KILM/ & AR

TOPOGRAPHY
WALKS
PLACE NAMES

Compiled by
Chris Morrison

PAISLEY
The Grian Press
2007

First published 2007

isbn
10: 0-9547996-9-0
13: 978-0-9547996-9-4

PREFACE

THE backbone of this work comes from a little book printed in Greenock in 1897 of walks around Kilmacolm with a simple yet interesting map (added here in sections). The author's identity is not apparent. We have added the entry for Kilmacolm from Francis Groome's definitive *Gazetteer of Scotland*, a note on old roads of Kilmacolm and a list of Kilmacolm place names from the Rev. James Murray's *Kilmacolm*, another list of Kilmacolm place names at the time of Pont, from *Timothy Pont's Renfrewshire* (courtesy of Alan Steel), some map detail from *Pont 33* (courtesy of the Trustees of The National Library of Scotland) as well as maps of Kilmacolm *et environs* from the *New Statistical Account*. An index of place names from the combined texts has been created.

The inspiration for the work comes from the local authority's new initiative of *Renfrewshire Leisure Lanes*. As one who has tramped around the network of leafy back-roads of old Renfrewshire for many years I am pleased that this wonderful resource has been identified and developed and hope that those who enjoy the charm of the Renfrewshire countryside around Kilmacolm *sans* a car will find the book useful. We must stress that much of the landscape has changed since the walks were compiled originally; they are now really of historical interest—in fact this is where much of their special appeal now lies. Some of the roads referred to are now busy roads and not suitable for leisure activities. Caution and common sense must prevail in using the guide. The Council's Planning Department should be able to advise on the current network of sign-posted leisure lanes as well as rights-of-way and access over what is considered to be private land.

Chris Morrison, Paisley 2007

KILMACOLM: TOPOGRAPHY, WALKS AROUND, PLACE NAMES

TOPOGRAPHICAL DESCRIPTION FROM GROOME'S GAZETTEER OF SCOTLAND

Kilmalcolm. A village and a parish in the Lower Ward of Renfrewshire. The village stands, 350 feet above sea-level, near the E border of the parish; and has a station on the Greenock and Ayrshire branch of the Glasgow and South-Western railway, 4 miles SE of Port Glasgow, 71/2 ESE of Greenock, and 15 WNW of Glasgow. It took its name, notwithstanding the modern spelling, from the dedication of its ancient church to St. Columba—Kil (cell) ma (my—fondly) colm (from the saint's baptismal name Colum, Latinized into Columba) meaning 'church or cell of my Colm.' A similar building up of a name is seen in Kilmaronock, 'church of my Ronock' (diminutive for St. Ronan). Its sheltered situation and the salubrity of its climate have led to a great extension during the last twenty years; and now it has a large number of tasteful villas, a post office under Paisley, with money order, savings bank, and telegraph departments, a branch of the Royal Bank, a good hotel, a large hydropathic establishment (1880), a gaswork, and water-works, formed in 1878 at a cost of nearly £5000, with a reservoir holding 1,500,000 gallons, and fed from Blacketty Burn. There is a public reading-room and a public park, both of which were presented to the village by Mr. Birkmyre, and an excellent golf-course. The parish church is a handsome edifice of 1833 (repaired in 1886), with a tower, and adjoins the aisle of a previous church, containing the tomb of the Earls of Glencairn, to the memory of whom a brass tablet memorial was erected in 1892 by their descendant, R.B. Cunningham-Graham of Gartmore. In 1890 the ruined chancel of the original parish church, which probably dated from the 12th century, was restored to serve as a vestry. There are a Free and a U.P. church. Pop. (1871) 395, (1881) 1170, (1891) 1634.

The parish is bounded N by Port Glasgow and the Firth of Clyde, E by Erskine and Houston, SE by Kilbar-chan, S by Lochwinnoch, SW by Largs in Ayrshire, and W by Innerkip and Greenock. Its utmost length, from NE to SW, is 61/2 miles; its breadth, from E to W, varies between 2 and 73/4 miles; and its area is 20,4053/4 acres, of which 2631/2 are foreshore and 4771/4 water. The coast-line, 21/2 miles in extent, is fringed by the low platform of the Firth's ancient sea-margin, and backed by pleasant braes 300 to 648 feet high. Gryfe Water, issuing from Gryfe reservoir on the Greenock border, flows southeastward right across the parish; and by it, Green Water, and its other affluents, the interior has been so channelled as to offer a charming variety of gentle hill and vale, with loftier moss and moorland to the W and S. Sinking along the Gryfe in the extreme E to 180 feet above sea level, the surface thence rises to 570 feet at Craiglunscheoch, 853 at Hardridge Hill, and 1446 at Creuch Hill. The predominant rocks are eruptive; and the soil on the low grounds is mostly light and gravelly, on the higher is moorish or mossy. About a half of the entire area is in tillage, plantations cover some 125 acres, and the rest of the land is either pastoral or waste. Mansions, noticed separately, are Duchall, Finlaystone, Carruth, and Broadfield. Kilmalcolm is in the presbytery of Greenock and synod of Glasgow and Ayr; the living is worth £535. Kilmalcolm and West Syde public schools, with respective accommodation for 632 and 67 children, have an average attendance of over 270 and 25, and grants of about £310 and £30. Pop. (1881) 2708, (1891) 3649.— *Ord. Sur.*, sh. 30, 1866. See Matthew Gemmill's *Kilmalcolm, Past and Present.*

KILMACOLM: PONT 33

Timothy Pont. Renfrewshire. [ca.1583-1596].   [NLS
shelfmark: Adv.MS.70.2.9 (Pont 33)]

Map reproduced by permission of the Trustees of The
National Library of Scotland

Renfrewshire c. 1840

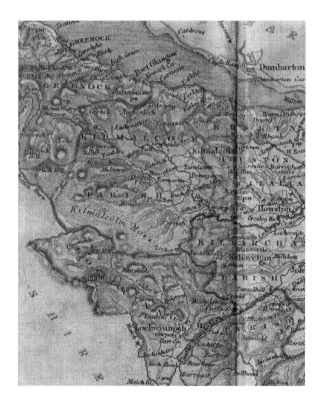

From The New Statistical Account: Renfrewshire

OLD ROADS AROUND KILMACOLM
(From James Murray's *Kilmacolm.*)

Very few of the old rough tracks, that served as roads
before the time of statute labour, can now be certainly
identified. The most easily traced, perhaps because it was
most used, was the path to the shore. Leaving the village
near the station it ran towards Auchenbothie, thence by
Gryfeside and Mathernock across the hill to Devol,
reaching Port-Glasgow near the present dock. Another
path, starting from the same point, but soon diverging to
the right, followed the line of Planetreeyetts, Leperston,
the Port-Glasgow dams, and reached the old Glasgow
Road near the south lodge of Finlaystone. Still another
path led directly north from the village past the manse
and crossed the moss to Kilallan, where the road diverged
to Houston and Bridge-of-Weir. There must have been
also a road of some kind, though I find no trace of it in
any old map, to Duchal Castle, and thence through the
Greenwater valley to Cairncurran perhaps also across
Duchal moor to Lochwinnoch. The present Bridge-of-
Weir Road-known of old as "Dennistoun Gait," an
ancient name that might well be preserved formerly followed a line somewhat to the west of the present road for
about a mile from the village. A turnpike road was made
about a century ago from Port-Glasgow to Kilbarchan,
leaving the old road at the Boglestane, and proceeding
through Kilmacolm to Bridge-of-Weir. The former road
from Port-Glasgow along the line of the railway must
have turned slightly to the right before reaching Auchenbothie, and entered the village to the west of the station.

WALKS AROUND KILMACOLM
INTRODUCTION.

A TRAVELLER alighting at a station in the North, stretched himself to breathe the fresh hill air, and exclaimed, "Is not this invigorating?" to which the porter replied, "No, sir; it is Inveramsay." The remark may be freely made at Kilmalcolm Station, and is often made, with no fear of misunderstanding. And yet the name of our village is perplexing too, and frequently the second remark made by visitors is, "By the way, how do you pronounce the name of this place?" The answer is that two ways are in use, but that which omits the middle l and accents the last syllable is the popular one, perhaps because it is more musical.

Another perplexing question is that of the Points of the Compass. The Hydropathic lies N.E. from the Station, so that the village between these points is somewhat askew—to the N. and S. line. However, the Railway Line, as it leaves the village towards Glasgow, runs due South, and gives a good guide to the eye; and the Parish Church stands East and West, and the old village street behind it runs due North, continuing to the Finlayston Road.

The principal roads leaving Kilmalcolm are those to Lochwinnoch (8 miles), crossing the railway at the station; to Bridge-of-Weir (4 miles); and to Port-Glasgow (4 miles); these last forming the main road running N.W. and S.E. through the village. Besides these there are four others; that passing the Public Park, and those to Finlayston, Bishopton, and Houston. The three high roads will be referred to by the initials *L., B. W.*, and *P. G.* The plan of the following pages is to describe first the shorter walks, from two to five miles in total length, in the order in which they might with advantage be taken by visitors; and afterwards a few longer excursions.

SHORT WALKS

1.—The Beech Hedges.

Go out by the *L.* Road one mile to the old toll. From here in fine weather Ben Lomond can be seen to the North. At the toll, turn to the left, past Milton Farm (*l.*) You go along a sheltered road, with well-kept hedges, till you reach a lodge on the right, where you cross the avenue to Duchal. (The u in Duchal is pronounced as in duck.) Then you cross the Gryfe, and pass the Mote Hill (*r*), one of the few remnants of antiquity, and the ruins of a croft; the road goes under the railway, and rises to the exposure of the *B.W.* high road, about a mile from Kilmalcolm. The wires which run along this walk are telephone wires, and are of copper. It is a three miles' walk.

2.—The Moss.

The first-mentioned walk is a sheltered one; but this second allows you to get all the weather there is. Indeed, after much rain it must be avoided, for part of the way is apt to be marshy. The Moss lies on the high ground above the village to the East. Coming up from the Post Office towards the Hydropathic, where the road divides into three, take the central one. That to the left goes to the

Hydropathic, and the right hand road leads to the Golf Course. The Moss Road winds up the hill between hedges like those of an English lane, passing the Parish Manse (*r*). At the top of the hill you come out upon the Moor through a gate. To the left below you is the Moss, a safe and extensive skating-ground in winter (Season Ticket, 2/-). On the right, by leaving the path for a few steps, a fine view can be had of the village and valley lying below you. The path keeps up from the water's edge at first, and if the day is fine you will feel that it would be easy to be good if you lived here. Presently you cross a stile below a plantation, and the path goes to the level of the water, and there are stepping-stones. These are in the parish of Houston. The stile is the boundary. The path then crosses two fields and comes out into the Houston Road. Turning back by the road, you pass the Golf Course and come down upon the *B.W.* Road, and so home; a walk of less than two miles.

3.—Leperston.

It would be well for the third walk to take quite a new direction. Go out the Finlayston Road, *i.e.*, the continuation of the old village street, behind the Parish Church, for about a mile. It is a hill at first, as you pass Watery-etts, and Planetreeyetts (*l*) and Old Hall (*r*); by-and-bye you reach a level. At some trees turn down to the left, between the two sections of the Port-Glasgow reservoir. Leperston Farm is on the left; then the ruins of Cloak; and, looking back, you can see Dumbarton Rock on a clear day. You emerge at the top of the hill upon the main *P.G.* Road, two miles from home. This is a good constitutional four-miles' walk, and is suitable for a wet day, if you have a waterproof, and would be cross if you stayed indoors.

4.—Slates.

To have a view of Kilmalcolm from the West, as it lies against its hills, go out past the railway station and across the Gryfe at Pacemuir Mill, to just where a milestone marks 3/4 of a mile from the village. Here turn into a *cul-de-sac* of hedges to your right; there is a gate and a farm road. You pass a well, six trees, and the outline in the grass of the ruins of Bridgend Farm. If you follow the cart track up the hill, and look back, you get a good view of our village. You come out upon a public road at Slates Farm. Here, under an ash tree at the gate, are to be seen two granite boulders, (This information is due to A. Laird, Esq., Caerleon.) intruders on the whinstone of the district, and doubtless brought from the North by a glacier. Return by Mount Blow and the Old Toll. 21/2 miles.

5.—Finlayston.

When the ground is dry, or frozen, there is a capital walk over the fields by an old right-of-way to Langbank. Turn to the right at the top of the old village street, by the Bishopton Road; and just behind the Hydropathic cross the dyke into the field on the left by stone steps. The path goes behind the gardens of a row of houses (*r*), and leads clearly enough along one dyke side for several fields, passing Old Hall to the left, till you descend a slope and cross on stepping-stones the marshy head waters of Dargavel Burn. At this point the track is often not to be found, but the point to aim at is a dyke that leads up the hill to a wood before you to the right. There you will find the path again, and it brings you out upon a country road opposite Gallahill Cottage. Below the cottage another footpath leads down to an East and West road, from which Langbank Station (Caledonian) can be reached, one mile to the right. To go all the way to Langbank and back would exceed the five-mile limit, and it would be a still longer walk to turn to the right at Gallahill and reach the Bishopton Road at Yetston. But if you keep to the road at Gallahill, and go down to the left, you come to Finlayston smithy and lodge, and then you are only a little over two miles from Kilmalcolm by the hilly but interesting Finlayston Road. The round is about five miles.

6.—St. Fillan's Church, Kilallan.

Half a mile from the Post Office along the *B.W.* Road, a country road to Houston leads up the hill to the left. You pass between the two Rowantreehill Farms, cross the Golf Course; after reaching the level the Moss Road comes in on the left—an alternative way of taking this walk. The ruined farm on the left is Elphiston; with West Glen behind. In dry weather it is possible to make one's way across the moor by Elphiston to the Bishopton Road. Keeping on the Houston Road you pass Lawfield (*1*), and at the bottom of the hill lies Kilallan, a farmhouse which was in former times the parish manse. Enter by the farm road to the churchyard and ruined church behind. On a slab on the wall may he read an interesting account of a former minister, Mr. Hutcheson. The last minister of Kilallan, at the time of its incorporation with Houston, was Mr. Menteith, grandfather of Principal Douglas of the Glasgow Free Church College. This is a walk of two miles each way. As to the double title above it should be explained that Fillan and Allan are one and the same name.

7.—The Orphan Homes.

To make a visit to The Homes with the least possible walking it is a good plan to take the train to Bridge of Weir. From there you have a walk of 13/4 miles, passing between the grounds of Torr (*l*) and Craigbet (*r*). You have then about three miles further to go to reach Kilmalcolm, either by Hattrick, Pomillan and *L.* Road, or take the first turning to the right and come in by the *B.W.* Road. The Orphan Homes proper occupy the most of what was Nittingshill Farm, acquired about 20 years ago by Mr. Quarrier for this purpose. More recently, Carsemeadow Farm, nearer to Bridge of Weir, has been added, and here a home for the treatment of consumption has been built, with offices and ventilating shaft at a little distance. Visitors are shewn through The Homes on weekdays, and may attend the church along with the children on Sabbaths. Hours of service—11 a.m. and 3 p.m. in winter; 6 p.m. in Summer. A capital view of The Homes, and of a great stretch of country besides, is got from a high part of the *B.W.* Road, about a mile and a quarter from Kilmalcolm. This view has been appropriately named Pisgah, and makes a good turning point for a short walk. Duchal House lies in its woods below.

8.—Kilbarchan.

A visit to Kilbarchan, famous for right-of-way and weaving, may be counted among the short walks by taking train to Bridge of Weir and back. You keep up the hill, passing above the Established Church, cross the Locher Burn at Penneld Bridge, and come down a steep hill past the grounds of Glentyan Ho. into Kilbarchan (11/2, miles). The objects of interest here are, handloom weaving of ornamental patterns in the cottages; the statue of Habbie Simpson, a strolling musician, on the front of the town hall; a Secession Church with a large burying ground; and the public park. You can leave the village close to where you entered it, but by a less steep hill, and you pass on the right the new public park, quite a rough hillside, but very suitable for the purposes of a common. At the foot of the hill turn to the left. It is perhaps two miles to Bridge of Weir station by the lower road.

9.—Netherwood.

To return to walks more strictly "near Kilmalcolm" we have still a great deal of country to explore towards the West, in the low ground on this side of the Side Hills, and on the high ground beyond. A very level walk is afforded by the Park Road. Take the third turning to the right beyond the railway station; to the left is the Public Park, with its eagle and lion, presented to the village by Adam Birkmyre, Esq., of Shalott, in 1890. Mr. Birkmyre's house is on the right. In a field with grassy knolls (r) was formerly situated Little Castle Hill farm, but the fields on both sides of the road now belong to Knockbuckle (l). The burn you cross at a plantation is the one which rises in The Moss and comes down through the village. About a mile out the road divides; turn to the left, cross the Gryfe, and join the Slates Road. The square house to the left is Netherwood. Return by the old Toll, three miles in all. Although the Slates Road lies on the N.E. side of a hill, it is sheltered in some winds, honeysuckle grows wild along it, and it commands a pleasant view of the village and country.

10.—Blacksholme.

There are seven different ways of reaching this farm from the village. The simplest way is to go out by the Park Road, cross the Gryfe (*1*), and at the top of the hill turn to the right. You reach Blacksholme (r) half a mile further on. The road then goes down to the Gryfe and crosses it, and immediately afterwards you can take a farm road to the right and return by the water side. This road leads to Auchenbothie, from which you can return to Kilmalcolm either by the Park or the *P.G.* Road. Less than four miles.

11.—Auchenbothie.

Leave the village by the *P.G.* Road, in front of the Parish Church. It brings you quickly clear of the houses, as there is no feuing in this direction yet. Half a mile out (*1*) above the railway is the "sliding rock," supposed to be smoothed by glacial action. Nearly opposite is the new Cemetery.

A mile from the village the road divides. Keeping on the main road to the right you pass a ruined croft, Craigmarlock (*1*), and East Kilbride, and may return by Leperston, four miles. (No. 3.)

The left hand road at the parting leads along the railway line. Cross either of the two bridges to Auchenbothie Farm. From there you can reach Blacksholme, or return by the Park Road (21/2 miles), or by Slates. (3 miles.)

12.—Gryfeside.

Instead of crossing the railway to Auchenbothie, in the last walk, keep on by the road beside the line till you pass under the railway to the left. On the right hand a farm road leads to Pennytersel; and on the same side is Mote Hill, one of four of that name in the neighbourhood; and in the distance Priestside Farm. Turn off the road down to the left; you pass Gryfeside (*r*) and reach the bridge at Blacksholme, where you have a choice of ways, by Auchenbothie, or the Park Road, or the Slates Road. Four miles.

13.—Old Duchal.

The remaining short walks are on the high ground behind the Side Hills. Go out by the Lochwinnoch or Station Road, and turn to the right at the Toll. At a gate on the right before you reach the Toll there is an alternative path through the fields. At the white house (Mount Blow) keep to the left, following the telephone wires. Turn down at the Green Farm (*l*) half a mile further on, by a rough, steep road to the Old Castle. The stream you cross at the foot of the hill is the Greenwater, named probably from the farm. Everyone is at liberty to enter the wood and explore the ruins. Below the Castle the two streams which surround it join.

It is worth while to continue on past the Castle till you emerge upon the Lochwinnoch and Greenock Road; cross it, and go up a cart road to Horseward; and still further to the ruins of High Craiglinsheoch. The prospect from here down the valley is a magnificent one; and you find yourself on the edge of the moor; you are far from cities; the sight of their smoke in the distance only helps by contrast to enhance your enjoyment of the purely rustic scenery beside you.

To this point and back the distance is perhaps slightly more than five miles.

14.—Margaret's Mill.

Instead of turning down at the Green Farm keep on by the telephone wires to a little beyond the next farm. Turn down to the left, a cart road, to the mill upon the Greenwater. Above the mill there are small waterfalls.

By keeping along the road a little further you reach the Side School (*r*) and Gateside (*l*.) Here you come into the old high road between Greenock and Lochwinnoch; turning to the left you pass Craiglinsheoch (*r*) and Horseward; and you can come home past Old Duchal. This makes a round of five miles and a half.

15.—Woodend.

Going by Old Duchal as in No. 13, turn to the left when you reach the Greenock Road. Nearly a mile along, past Blackwater Farm (*r*), turn down to the left to the gamekeeper's house, then through the wood to the right. No dogs must be taken by this way. You come out of the wood at Woodend Cottage, and join the *L.* Road below at the Stepend's Smithy and bridge. Five miles.

16.—Killochries.

Take the *L.* Road as far as Stepends—the smith's shop and bridge; and enter by a gate an old road opposite the smith's cottage. At the head of the road turn to the right, and you presently see carved stone gate pillars (*l*) as if of an old mansion. Here in a park there are daffodils in spring; and here at this date (1897) is to be found the oldest inhabitant of the district, Mr. Orr. Passing on, turn to the left at the next farm, Newton; and so to Glenmill (*r*); again take the road to the left, and instead of following it down all the way, cross a stile (*l*) above what was once a school, and is now a gamekeeper's cottage, and rejoin the *L.* Road by a field path. Returning home you pass Mains of Duchal, and an avenue and lodge, both to the right. Five miles.

There are other walks in this direction, up to Lakeston, beyond Glenmill; to Barnshake, beyond Newton; and round from Killochries, turning to the right at Newton, and home by Old Duchal or Gateside; each of these may be counted to be a walk of about six miles. Again, following the *L.* Road to the third bridge, at; Pomillan, and taking the first turn to the left, there is a round by Hattrick (*1*), and near the Orphan Homes, which is not much over five miles.To go to Bridge-of-Weir by this road is about five miles; and a train can be got to return by every hour.

WALKS OF SIX MILES AND MORE

Those who are able to make longer excursions are not so dependent upon a guide book. The routes now indicated may serve as an introduction to the neighbourhood.

1.—The Boglestone.

On the road side (*1*) above Clune Brae Toll, a mile out of Port-Glasgow, are to be seen built into a wall the fragments of a stone, once apparently a landmark. It will serve as the destination of a walk, because you can go to it by the main *P.G.* Road (3 miles); there is a fine prospect both on the way and as you descend the "Brae;" and you can return below Broadfield House to Finlayston (2 miles), along what is like an avenue rather than a public road. Here also there are beautiful glimpses of the Clyde. At Finlayston there is to be seen a remnant of a very old Yew Tree under which John Knox dispensed the Sacrament in both kinds, using inverted silver candlesticks for cups. In returning to Kilmalcolm (2 miles), the highest part of the road is 500 feet above the Clyde, so that it is not to be wondered at if the gradient is steep. Seven miles. You can return straight from the Boglestone by the higher road, near to the railway. Six miles.

2.—Barochan Cross.

Behind Kilallan Church (two miles: see Short Walks) there is a road to the left, off the Houston Road, which brings you in two miles more to the Houston and Greenock High Road. There on an eminence in a field stands an old stone cross—a cart road leads up to it. It is believed to have been erected in memory of a young man from across the Clyde who fell in a local battle. Figures of men and horses can still be seen in the worn carving. Going towards Houston (1 mile) you can pass through the village and reach Bridge-of-Weir (1 1/2 miles), and so return (10 miles.) Or, by the more hilly road to the right before reaching Houston, return by Kilallan; making a round of nine miles.

3.—Bishopton.

The road which turns up the hill to the right at the head of the village street, and runs behind the Hydropathic, is a pleasant one for the first mile; but after you pass behind the Craigmuir Hill it becomes so unpromising that one would be apt to turn back. But if you hold on for nearly two miles down the long Dargavel Glen, you will be rewarded. You come out from the moor at last upon the smiling lowlands of Erskine and Houston parishes, studded over with mansion houses and their grounds.

At the turnpike road go to the left, then to the right at the Old Toll; and one more turn to the right and to the left brings you to Bishopton (5½ miles.) But if you keep on along the turnpike you come by-and-bye within sight of the Clyde opposite Dumbarton. You may visit the West Ferry and Langbank; and return to Kilmalcolm by a choice of three ways. (1). Right over Barscube Hill, and so back into the Dargavel Glen Road. (2). By the Gallahill right-of-way (Short Walks, No. 5.) (3). By the Finlayston Road. Eleven miles; and fourteen if you go round by Bishopton.

A shorter round is obtained by leaving the Glen Road to the left, crossing Barscube Hill, and returning by either of the Finlayston Roads, or back from Gallahill into the Glen Road again. Ten miles.

4.—Gryfe Castle.

Besides the Barochan Road and the Houston Road at Kilallan, there is a third going off to the right from the Houston Road, a little beyond the old church. Following it you come down upon the end of Bridge-of-Weir village, and so home by Gryfe Castle Seven miles. On the Lodge are to be read these words—

Gif ye did as ye sud, ye sail haf as ye wud.

5.—Carruth Woods.

Going out by the *L.* Road you come at the third milestone to Carruth gate. After this the road ascends through the finest woods in the district. To the left, after passing Carruth, a road leads down towards Bridge-of-Weir,

passing the new Home for Consumptives and Torr Hall
(*1*). You may go on to Bridge-of-Weir and return by the
high road (9 miles); or, doubling round Torr Hall, by
Craigbet and the Homes (8 miles).

6.—Auchencloich and Barnbeth.

By following the Carruth Road a mile further, another
capital walk can be had. Just where a bridge over the
Locher water would take you into Lochwinnoch parish,
turn to the left along a grassy road, so little used is it.
Presently the road rises still higher till at Auchencloich
you will feel that it is quite unnecessary to go to Switzer-
land to breathe exhilarating mountain air. Take the next
turning to the left, skirting a large moss, Barmuflloch
Dam; passing Barnbeth and Clavens you have a long
downhill to Bridge-of-Weir; a nine miles walk. And if
you have taken the precaution to start before 3 p.m., and
to walk smartly, you may catch the 5.30 train and be
home in time for tea at 6.

7.—Devol and Mathernock.

There is an even more exciting walk, of a similar
length, across the moor above Port-Glasgow. Take the
P.G. Road, either of them, but that by the railway is
directest. After three miles turn to the left, under the line,
and then for a mile further to the head of Barr's Brae.
Here go up the farm road, past Devol and the Golf
Course. By and bye the road becomes very rough with
rocks and ruts; but it is high, and the rough walking adds
to the enjoyment of it. Pass through a gate to the left. You
come out on the High Greenock Road beyond Mathernock, and return by the *P.G.* Road.

8. —Greenock.

The walk to Greenock is worth taking if only for the two miles of it above Port-Glasgow looking down on the Clyde. Below, in the James Watt Dock, you may sometimes see the three black funnels of the s.s. City of Rome. There is always shipping at the Tail-of-the-Bank. Beyond that you see the Gareloch; and up the river there is a beauty of another kind.

Leaving Kilmalcolm by the *P.G.* Road you go under the railway as if going to Gryfeside (Short Walk, No. 32) Instead of turning down, keep on past Priestside (*r*) and Mathernock (*l*). At 33/4 miles you join the telephone wires, which have come round by the Gateside way. A mile or so further on you see the Clyde.

Here, before the road turns away to the left, you may leave it by a footpath across a field and visit Wallace's Leap (*r*), a waterfall and a rock in the Devol Burn. It is certain that the rock was there in the time of Wallace. In the burn below the fall may be seen boulders imbedded in volcanic ash. (Mr. Alex Laird)

When Greenock is reached, a short cut to the station may be taken by not going under the railway, but keeping it still on the right. You come down upon the railway bridge at Lynedoch station. The distance is seven miles.

9.—Dunrod Hill.

A conspicuous object in the horizon, looking from Kilmalcolm, is Corlich Hill (994 feet). It is climbed from the Greenock Road at the head of the Devol Burn, and the view from it is very commanding. But a still finer view is to be had from a smaller hill, Dunrod (973 feet). It lies on the way to Inverkip, to the right.

On reaching the junction of the roads to Greenock, just described (33/4 miles), go a little way to the left, and then to the right, along the Gryfe stream and reservoir. It is a genuine moor road for four miles, passing Garshangan (*r*) and Garvock (*r*), along the Gryfe reservoir and then Loch Thom (so called after a Mr. Thom who had to do with bringing its water into Greenock). At the S. end of Loch Thom, the left hand road goes to Largs (16 miles), the other doubles back along the water and then down by a wooded dale to Inverkip (12 Miles). Near where it leaves the reservoir you may go down by wooden steps to a path along the Cut, or Aqueduct; and both while following its course, and especially by leaving it to climb Dunrod Hill, magnificent views are obtained. Ailsa Craig is sometimes visible to the South, and many snow-clad peaks to the North.

Going on by the road to Inverkip there is a Roman Bridge, near old Dunrod Castle; and at the village itself a picturesque glen; while the woods and parks of Ardgowan House lie before you on the opposite slope. Return by rail to Upper Greenock, and then from Lynedoch station to Kilmalcolm.

10.—Carncurran Hill.

This hill has no view to speak of, but it is curiously formed on its summit, and is easily climbed, Leave the Inverkip Road just described at Dykefoot (4 miles from Kilmalcolm), and go by the fields. Descend on the south side to Hillside Farm, and from there by the farm road return to Faulds and Gateside. Nine miles. It is around of about eight miles to go out by the Gateside Road and come in by Mathernock.

11.—Cauldside.

Go out to Mathernock by the *P.G.* and Greenock Road (No. 8); turn sharply to the left; cross the Gryfe, a very small stream here; the farm on the left as you go up the rough hill road is Cauldside. To the right is Horse-craigs, and by its farm road you can make a round and join the high road; or, keep on, over the shoulder of the Side Hill (600 feet); it is a pleasant hill to climb at this end of it, with grassy turf and rocks; and join the high road at Chapel, thence home by Gateside. Seven miles.

12.—Waterworks.

Go out by Old Duchal (Short Walks, No. 13), and on reaching the Greenock Road beyond it turn to the left, and presently again to the right, before the road descends to cross the Blackwater. This is a country road—one of the few road-sides where blaeberries ripen—leading first to the old reservoir (*l*), and then a mile further to the new one (4 miles.) Here might have been seen, before operations began, three burns uniting, one of them with dainty little cascades; and at the bottom of the dell the stream they formed ran under overhanging rocks, with great clumps of fern for miniature forests. Now, alas! pick and shovel have made the fairy glen into the bed of a commonplace pond. Below the old reservoir, however, and above Old Duchal, there are picturesque reaches of the burn.

13.—Lochwinnoch.

The *L.* Road leaves Kilmalcolm by the railway bridge, and for the first half mile is lined on the right hand side by houses. You cross the Gryfe at Pacemuir Mill—a name taken from the farm on the left, close to the village.

For five miles the road is divided into sections by the burns it crosses; the Gryfe at the Mill; the Greenwater at Stepend's Smithy; the Mill Burn at Pomillan; the Gotter Water at Bridgeflat, and then 41/2 miles out, on the high ground, the Locher Water, at Barnbroak. These streams furrow the country like a fan, and all flow into the Gryfe.

Between Pomillan and Bridgeflat you are alongside of the Orphan Homes (*l*), and look over the fields to them. By the roadside (*r*) stands Knockbuckle, famed for its honey. Although no bees are to be seen by the passer by, there are many hives of them; but they are too busy to loiter about. Where the road crosses the Gotter Water, at Bridgeflat, there are three streams on the one side of the road, and only one on the other. The bridge is at the confluence. At Carruth Gate (3 miles) the road begins to ascend, and continues to do so for about a mile, through woods. These woods are the chief feature of the walk. Afterwards you are for some miles at a very high level, till you come down into the valley of the Calder, and reach Lochwinnoch (8 miles.) If you wish to return by train, it is well to remember that the station is a mile beyond the town, and make allowance.

At Chapelton Toll (6 miles) a road to the left will take you by Burntshiels to Kilbarchan (4 miles further), or direct to Bridge-of-Weir, about the same distance.

14.—Misty Law.

This is the finest excursion of all from Kilmalcolm. Those who cycle or drive have to go by the *L.* Road to Boghead (71/2 miles), half a mile from Lochwinnoch, and then turn to the right up the valley of the Calder (4 miles more); but this is a long detour. At Knockbuckle House (21/2 miles), take a country road to the right, then

immediately turn to the left, and go on past Wraes
Cottage, and so up by the Gotter Water as far as the road
will serve you to the ruin of Bridgeflat Ward. Then you
must continue up the burn by whatever track you can
find, and at last take to the heather, and climb Craigminnin (900 feet), from the top of which you will see how far
you have still to go. Between this and the Windy Hill, or
Green Hill (1,000 feet), lies a peat-moss; and here on the
boundary of Kilmalcolm and Lochwinnoch parishes
meetings of Covenanters used to be held. Cross the top,
or the right hand shoulder of the Green Hill, and descend
to the right hand side of a plantation. You strike the road
between Muirshiels House and a Mill higher up the
Calder, where there is a bridge. You are now a little over
six miles from home, but the last three of these being
over the hills, may count as four. You most naturally get
on to the hillside of Queen's Seat Hill, but should take
the first opportunity of crossing the Raith Burn (*1*) on to
Misty Law. From the summit, if the air is clear, there is
nothing else in the way to prevent you from seeing Ailsa
Craig and all Ayrshire to the south, and the northern hills,
Ben Cruachan and Ben More. Return by Craigminnin; or,
proceeding down the Calder by the Muirshiels Road for
two miles, cross the moor at Kairm Dam, and regain the
L. Road five miles from home.

The phrase used to be, "out of the world and into
Kilmalcolm." To make this still true the visitor must not
stop at the village of that name, but go out of *its* world
into the world of nature round about. The resources of the
social life of Kilmalcolm are undoubtedly great, yet as
the Paisley woman said, "Folks has their troubles here

the same as ither places," and one way of getting the
better of troubles is to take a long walk in the country.

> 0 world, as God has made it, all is beauty;
> And knowing this is love, and love is duty;
> What further can be sought for, or declared?

If the directions given above help visitors more quickly
to feel at home in the district, the aim of this Handbook
will have been accomplished.

KILMACOLM PLACE NAMES.

(From James Murray's *Kilmacolm*)

THE examination of local place-names, and the attempt to find their original significance, is a branch of study, which, though beset with difficulties, is of fascinating interest. Fragments of real history are imbedded in these names, waiting to be excavated and pieced together by the patient investigator. There is a curious persistency about them, especially those that describe physical features, such as hills and streams. The race that gave the names may pass away, but their successors continue to use them, though often strangely altering their form, through ignorance of their meaning, or through organic inability to catch the original pronunciation. Thus, it is four or five centuries at least since the parishioners of Kilmacolm were a Gaelic-speaking population; and yet the names that are applied to-day to the surrounding hills, to the burns and streamlets, to the farms and fields, are prevailingly Gaelic. In the case of some, the modifications they have undergone are so great that it is extremely difficult to identify them. But, for the most part, the pronunciation has suffered less in this way than the spelling; and in almost every case the former is a much more reliable guide than the latter.

The first name that calls for attention is naturally that of the parish itself. Its meaning is perfectly clear, nor would it ever have been questioned but for a change in the ancient spelling of the name, which was gradually adopted, when it became "Kilmalcolm." The facts of the case are simply these. From the earliest documentary record in which the name occurs, the confirmation by

Florence, Bishop of Glasgow, in 1202, down to the end of the seventeenth century, it is invariably spelled Kilmacolm, with the occasional variants, Kilmacolme, Kilmakolm, Kylmacolm, Kylmacolme, Killmacolm, Kilmacom, etc. It so appears in the Register of the Abbey of Paisley, in the Rental Roll of the Abbey, in the Diocesan Registers of Glasgow, and indeed, in all contemporary documents in which it occurs. So also in the manuscript records of the Presbytery of Paisley, in which the name is necessarily written hundreds of times, it is not till almost the end of the seventeenth century that the form Kilmalcolm is found. Thereafter the forms are used indifferently till we reach modern times, when Kilmalcolm becomes stereotyped. In the Poll-Tax Rolls of 1695, the form adopted is "Killmacomb," which is also uniformly used in Crookshank's *History*, published in 1749. In the Kirk-Session Records, from the beginning of the eighteenth century, the middle "l" is usually inserted.

But with this variation in the spelling, the pronunciation remained unchanged. The accent was always on the last syllable. Sir Herbert Maxwell, the Rhind lecturer in 1893, says:—"I will ask you to pause for a moment on Kilmalcolm, for railway influence, I am sorry to say, is prevailing to corrupt it into Kilmalcolm. The second "l" is no part of the name; in the twelfth century it was rightly written Kilmakolme. *Ma*, or *mo*, is an endearing prefix to a saint's name." (Scottish Land Names) The mispronunciation to which he refers never really took hold; and there is little excuse for the author of the *Fasti* being so far misled by it as to state: "the church was dedicated to Malcolm III. of Scotland." Cosmo Innes, in his *Origins Parochiales*, rightly says that this dedication to King Malcolm is without any authority. "There can be little doubt," he adds, "that it was one of the numerous churches dedicated to St. Columba." The etymology is indeed unmistakeable. It is simply the Gaelic, "Cill ma Coluim," the church of my own Columba. The present writer recently made an effort to have the original spelling restored, which, through the influential assistance of Sir C. Bine Renshaw, Sir Hugh Shaw Stewart, Sir Herbert Maxwell, and others, proved successful. The railway company, and all the public Boards in the county and parish, adopted the form "Kilmacolm," and last year the post office, with the authority of the Scotch Office, declared that henceforth this shall be the official spelling of the name.

Many of the names in the parish are simply English words, and need no explanation. Some of them are compounds of proper names, as Dennistoun, Finlaystone, Youngston, Lukeston, Blacksholm, Carsemeadow, Margaret's Mill, and Gibblaston. Others are manifestly suggested by their situation, or by some natural feature in the neighbourhood, as Rowantreehill, Birkenhill, Planetreeyetts, Bridgeflat, Overton, Yonderton, Woodend, Bogside, Dykefoot, Townhead, etc. But, besides these and the like, there is a considerable number of names that are either wholly or partly Gaelic, or otherwise present difficulty in their interpretation. All acquainted with the difficulty of tracing the origin of place-names will understand that many of the meanings here suggested are doubtful. The following list aims at being complete, excluding only names of quite recent origin. In some cases, it will be observed, we have not cared even to hazard a guess at the meaning. In many others, as I have said, no explanation is necessary.

1. NAMES OF ESTATES, FARMS, ETC.

Auchenbothie, field of the bothy, or hut.

Auchendores, field of waters.

Auchendrach, field of the bramble.

Auchenfoil, field of the wood, or of deceit.

Auchenleck, field of the flagstones.

Auchentiber, field of the well.

Balrossie, house on the promontory.

Bankbrae, a slope.

Barclaven, hill of the kite, the kestrel hawk.

Bardrainy, hill of the black thorns.

Barfill, St. Fillan's hill.

Barmoss, hill of the moss.

Barnbrock, hill of the badger.

Barnshake, hill of succour.

Bannockhill, shaped like bannock.

Baskethill, shaped like basket.

Bierhill, hill of barley.

Birkenhill, birch hill.

Blacksholm, Black's meadows.

Blackstoun, Black's house.

Blackwater, Duchal.

Bogside, the slope from the bog.

Brackenridge, ridge of the bracken ferns.

Braefauld, sheepfolds on the slope.

Braehead, head of the slope.

Branchal, or Branchill, perhaps Bruntshiels, the burnt dwellings.

Bridgend, at the end of the bridge.

Bridgeflat, flat lands at the bridge.

Broadfield, the wide field, or fold.

Butts, or Buits, croft, or butts for shooting at.

Burnbank, on the slope of the stream.

Burnside, by the side of the stream.

Cairncurran, the cairn of the cairns, or hill of rowans.

Cairnkebbuck, cheese shaped hill.

Carnappock.

Carruth. Carruthmuir.

Carseknowe, Kerr's hill, or hill beside the river.

Carsmeadow, Kerr's meadow, or meadow beside the river.

Castlehill, hill adjoining castle of Finlaystone.

Cauldside, cold slope.

Chapel, site of old chapel of Syde; also Denniston Chapel, near Finlaystone.

Clachers, a stony place.

Cloak, a large stone.

Corleck, the hill of flagstones.

Craigbet, the crag of birches.

Craigend's Dennistoun, part of Dennistoun belonging to Craigends.

Craiglunsheogh, crag of the ash trees.

Craigmarloch, robbers' crag.

Craigneuk, crag in the corner, or corner of crag.

Croftluton, croft let on lease, or (perhaps) Luton, a proper name.

Cunston, the cowane's, or dyker's house.

Devol, Davol, Davolsglen, perhaps devil's glen.

Dennistoun, house of Dennis or Denzil.

Dippany, Diffeny, the two pens or mounds, or twopenny land.

Dipps, probably contraction of Dippany.

Douglie.

Dubbs, pools.

Duchal, black water.

Dunfad, long hill.

Dykefoot, from dyke, a dry wall.

Eastside, on the east slope of the valley.

Faulds, sheepfolds.

Finlaystone, house of Finlay.

Garshangan.

Gateside, side of the road or gait.

Gibblaston, Gilbert's house.

Gills, narrow glen.

Glenmill, mill in the glen.

Gowkhouse, house of the cuckoo.

Green, sunny place.

Greenhill, sunny hill.

Gryfeside, side of Gryfe.

Hairlaw, hill of the hare.

Hardridge, hard ground.

Hattrick, Hattonridge; Hatton, proper name.

Heugh, rugged hill.

Hillside, on slope of hill.

Horsecraig, crag of the horses.

Horseward, shelter for horses.

Kilbride, cell of St. Bridget.

Killochries, scrub in which a boar lies, or Kinloch's cattle pens.

Kilmacolm, church of my Columba.

Knaps, hillocks.

Knockbuckle, hill of the cow-herd.

Knockmountain, hill of the hill, a tautology.

Ladymuir, moor of Our Lady.

Langrigs, long ridges.

Langside, long slope.

Law, hill.

Lawpark, park on the hill.

Laidentoun, house by the mill lade.

Leechfield, Leech, proper name, or field of leeches.
Leperstoun, lepers' house.
Littlemill.
Lukeston, Luke's house.
Mains, farm steading.
Margaret's mill, Mauldsmill, Moldsmill.
Mansfield.
Mathernock, middle hill.
Maukenhill, hill of the hare.
Maukenleisur, the hare's pasture.
Merryrigs.
Midton, the middle house.
Milton, the mill house.
Moss-side, the side of the marsh.
Montreal.
Mowdie Park, the mole's park.
Muiredge, edge of moor.
Muirhouse, house on moor.
Mutehill, hill of meeting.
Nethermains, lower farm steading.
Netherwood, lower wood.
Newark, Newwerk, new building.
Newton, new house.
Nittingshill, nutting hill.
Oldhall, old house.
Overmains, upper farm steading.
Overton, upper house.
Overwood, upper wood.
Pacemuir, on the edge of the moor.
Park.
Parkhill.
Parklee.
Pennytersal, penny lands.

Planetreeyetts, gates of the plane trees.

Pomillan, mill burn.

Priestside, priest's land.

Puddockhole, frog's hole.

Rountreehill, hill of the mountain ash.

Shells, dwelling or shieling.

Slates, slated house.

Slimure, Slaemuir, moor of the sloes.

Stepends, end of stepping stones over Duchal Burn.

Syde, hill.

Tandlebrae, slope of the sacred fire.

Torr, mound.

Townhead, at the head of the town or village.

Townside, house on the slope.

Wards, shelters.

Wardwell, well at the ward.

Wateryetts.

Westside, on the west slope.

Woodend.

Woodhead.

Woodside.

Wraes, Raess, enclosures for cattle.

Yetts, gates.

Yonderhill.

Yonderton.

Youngstoun, Young's house.

2. NAMES OF HILLS.

Cairncurran Hill.

Coplie, grey, cup-shaped hill.

Corleck, hill of flagstones.

Coward Hill.

Clune Brae, the slope of the haugh or meadow.

Craig of Todholes, crag of fox holes.
Craigminnen, crag of the young goats.
Creuch, hill.
Dunnairbuck, hill of the roe-buck.
Gallowhill, hill of gallows.
Gledhill, hill of kite.
Heddles, cords in a loom through which the warp is passed.
Hyndal.
Knockminwood, wood on the hill of the kids.
Knockmore, great hill.
Knocknairhill, knocknar, hill of slaughter.
Lurg, shin bone—hence "spur of a hill."
Lyles' Hill, hill of the Lyles of Duchal.
Millyouther, dun-coloured hill.
Smeath Hill.
Syde Hill, sith, a hill.
Whinny Hill, hill of whins or gorse.

3. NAMES OF STREAMS.
Blacketty, black water.
Carruth Burn.
Crankly Burn, twisting stream.
Duchal Water, black water.
Finlaystone Burn.
Gillburn, clear stream.
Gotter, a drain.
Locher, stream of rushes.
Millburn, Powmillan, mill stream.
Monyburn, many streams united.
Powmillan, mill burn.
Rottenburn, routing or brawling stream.
Spoutal, gushing stream.

Table 1: Pont 33 - Place Names of Kilmacolm

1	2	3
Achanachle	Gabblis-tou(n)	Kragunchach
Achinbuith	Gaimer-stou(n)	Laffild
Achinlem	Glen B	Laverokstain
Bamteth	Gryph fl	Lady moore
Barshag	Harig	Locchyr flu.
Blacksoom	Heuch	Macharnock
Brehead	Horscre.	Miltoun
Brigend	Horsewaird	Mony B.
Chapel of Syd	Housto(un)	Paneter
Coldsid	Karnkuren	Plaidfild
Creuch moore	B. of Kar-ruith	Pristsyde
Creuch	Karry Burns	Powmillen B
Crykhil	Kellarkrek	Resto(un)
Dennistoun	Kerruith	Torhil

Table 1: Pont 33 - Place Names of Kilmacolm

1	2	3
Ducchal	Kicma-kou(h)am	Wakmill
Duffald	Knaps	Watersid
Dugla Hil	Kraigbait	Woodend
Dupeny	Kraigbar	Woodhouse

UNDERNEATH: DIAGRAMMATIC MAP IN SECTIONS FROM THE 1897 GUIDE-BOOK

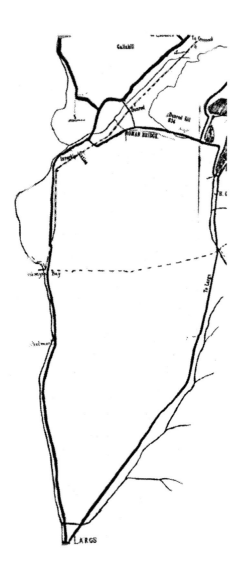

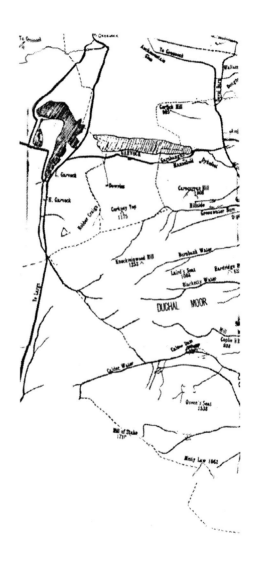

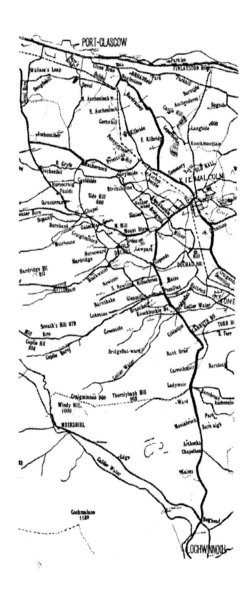

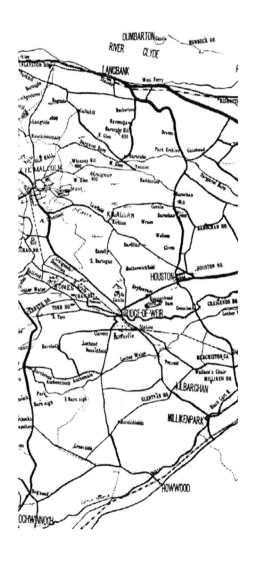

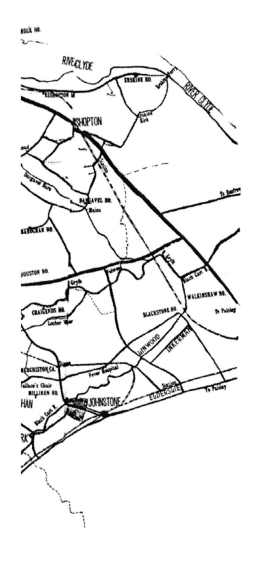

Printed in the United Kingdom
by Lightning Source UK Ltd.
121010UK00001B/303